Administrative and Logistic Responsibilities
for
DoD Dependents Schools

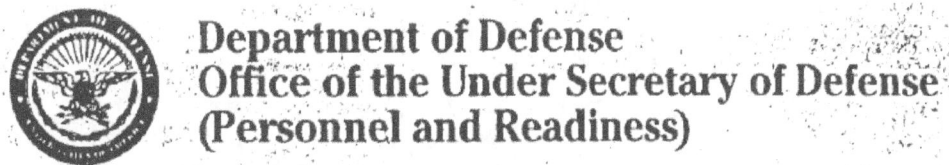

Department of Defense
Office of the Under Secretary of Defense
(Personnel and Readiness)

August 1995

ASSISTANT SECRETARY OF DEFENSE
4000 DEFENSE PENTAGON
WASHINGTON, D.C. 20301-4000

AUG 11 1995

FORCE MANAGEMENT POLICY

FOREWORD

This Manual is issued under the authority of DoD Directive 1342.6, "Department of Defense Dependents Schools (DoDDS)," October 13, 1992. It prescribes uniform procedures for the DoD Components to follow when providing administrative and logistic support to the DoDDS.

DoD 1342.6-M-1, "Administrative and Logistic Responsibilities for DoD Dependents Schools," October 1978, is hereby canceled.

This Manual applies to the Office of the Secretary of Defense (OSD), the Military Departments, the Chairman of the Joint Chiefs of Staff and the Joint Staff, the Unified and Specified Commands, the Defense Agencies, and the DoD Field Activities administratively supported by the OSD (hereafter referred to collectively as "the DoD Components"). To the extent that Military Services issuances or publications conflict with this Manual, this Manual shall govern.

This Manual is effective immediately and is mandatory for use by all the DoD Components. The heads of the DoD Components may issue supplementary instructions only when necessary to provide for unique requirements within their DoD Components. Such supplements must be coordinated and approved by the DoDDS before implementation.

Send recommended changes to the Manual through channels to:

> Department of Defense
> Office of Dependents Education
> 4040 N. Fairfax Drive
> Arlington, VA 22203-1635

The DoD Components may obtain copies of this Manual through their own publications channels. Other Federal Agencies and the public may obtain copies from the U.S. Department of Commerce, National Technical Information Service, 5285 Port Royal Road, Springfield, VA 22161.

F. Pang

TABLE OF CONTENTS

TABLE OF CONTENTS

APPENDICES

REFERENCES

(a) DoD Directive 1342.6, "Department of Defense Dependents Schools (DoDDS)," October 13, 1992

(b) Dependents Schools Regulation 5550.9, "Department of Defense Dependents Schools Compensation for Extra Duty Assignments," October 7, 1988

(c) DoD Instruction 4000.19, "Interservice, Interdepartmental, and Interagency Support," August 9, 1995

(d) DoD Directive 1015.5, "DoD Student Meal Program," October 11, 1983

(e) DoD Directive 1342.13, "Eligibility Requirements for Education of Minor Dependents in Overseas Areas," July 8, 1982

(f) DoD 4525.8-M, "DoD Official Mail Manual," July 1987, authorized by DoD Directive 4525.6, May 5, 1980

(g) DoD 4500.36-R, "Management, Acquisition, and Use of Motor Vehicles, "March 1994, authorized by DoD Directive 4500.36, April 10, 1985

(h) DoD Instruction 1010.13, "Provision of Medically Related Services to Children Receiving or Eligible to Receive Special Education in DoD Dependents Schools Outside the United States," August 28, 1986

(i) DoD Instruction 1342.12, "Education of Handicapped Children in the DoD Dependent Schools," December 17, 1981

(j) DoD Instruction 6205.1, "Immunization Requirements for DoD Dependents Schools, Section 6 Schools, and Day Care Centers Operated by the Department of Defense (HA)," May 29, 1985

(k) Defense FAR Supplement (DFARS), current edition

(l) DoD 4000.25-7-M, "Military Standard Billing System (MILBILLS)," January 1985

(m) Dependents Schools Manual 4100.2, "Material Management Manual," current edition

(n) Federal Acquisition Regulation, current edition

(o) DoD Directive 7150.5, "Responsibility for Programing and Financing Facilities at DoD Installations Utilized by Two or More DoD Components," August 26, 1978

(p) DoD Instruction 7040.4, "Military Construction Authorization and Appropriation," March 5, 1979

(q) DoD Instruction 4165.56, "Relocatable Buildings," April 13, 1988

(r) Joint Federal Travel Regulations, Volume 1, "Uniformed Service Members," current edition

(s) Joint Travel Regulations, Volume 2, "Department of Defense Civilian Personnel," current edition

(t) DoD 7220.9-M, "Department of Defense Accounting Manual," October 1983, authorized by DoD Instruction 7220.9, "DoD Accounting Policy," October 22, 1981

(u) NAVSUP PUB 437, "MILSTRIP/MILSTRAP," July 1991

(v) Naval Supply Systems Command Manual, Volume II, "Supply Ashore," February 1976, Reprinted August 3, 1990

(w) Memorandum of Understanding between the Department of the Navy and the DoD Office of Dependents Schools, "U.S. Navy Supply Support of Department of Defense Overseas Dependents Schools," June 16, 1976

(x) NAVCOMPT Manual, Volume III, "Appropriations, Cost, and Property Accounting (Field)," April 25, 1952

C1. CHAPTER 1

POLICY

C1.1. PURPOSE

This Manual implements DoD Directive 1342.6 (reference (a)), and assigns responsibilities for the administrative and logistic support of the DoDDS.

C1.2. MISSION

The DoDDS mission is to provide a quality educational program from kindergarten through grade 12 for eligible dependents of U.S. Military, DoD civilian, and other eligible personnel stationed in overseas areas, to provide a free appropriate public education for children with disabilities, age 3 to 21, and to operate a community college program for eligible dependents in Panama. The DoDDS has no authority to fund the education of an otherwise eligible DoD dependent unless the DoDDS has placed the child in a DoDDS or non-DoDDS school, or a court of competent jurisdiction or an impartial hearing officer has so ordered. Sponsors of eligible dependents are instructed to contact and obtain the approval of the appropriate DoDDS regional director before enrolling a student in a non-DoDDS school in locations where DoDDS does not operate schools.

C1.3. DEFINITIONS

C1.3.1. Curriculum. The academic program offerings in a school.

C1.3.1.1. Curricular activities. Organized activities sponsored by the school that are DIRECTLY RELATED to the established curriculum; for example, study trips.

C1.3.1.2. Co-Curricular activities. Organized activities sponsored by the school that generally take place after school hours, and are designed specifically to ENRICH AND SUPPLEMENT the academic program; such as the "Model United Nations Program," school sponsored clubs such as the Computer Club, the Future Business Leaders, and the Interscholastic Athletic and Academic Program. Compensation for these activities is administered in accordance with DS Regulation 5550.9, (reference (b)).

C1.3.2. <u>District Superintendent</u>.   An individual employed by the DoDDS to manage several schools in a defined geographical area referred to as a district.

C1.3.3. <u>Installation Commander</u>.   The commander of a DoD activity providing logistic and administrative support to DoDDS activities at a given location.   (The term "installation commander" encompasses "base commander," "community commander," or similar designations.)

C1.3.4. <u>Investment Costs</u>.   Costs incurred for construction and equipment, which are funded by construction or procurement appropriations, rather than Operation and Maintenance (O&M) appropriations.

C1.3.5. <u>Logistic and Administrative Support</u>.   That support includes common supplies, services, facilities, privileges, and benefits; and is grouped broadly into two categories, as follows:

C1.3.5.1. "<u>Agency Support</u>".   Agency support includes items furnished to an Agency or an organization, as contrasted to an individual.   Examples are real estate (for office or warehousing space), police and fire protection, utilities, registration of Agency vehicles, and communications services.

C1.3.5.2. "<u>Individual Support</u>".   Individual support includes items furnished to individuals, as opposed to Agencies or organizations.   Examples are: commissary and exchange privileges, registration of privately-owned vehicles (POVs), medical and dental services, use of recreational facilities (for example, theaters, clubs, libraries, craft shops, and athletic facilities), and local welfare and/or community services.

C1.3.6. <u>Non-DoDDS Schools</u>.   Schools, other than the DoDDS, approved by the respective DoDDS regional director, which may or may not require tuition payments for space-required students.

C1.3.7. <u>Other-Users Factor (OUF)</u>.   The percentage by which engineering, custodial, refuse collection, real property rental, utilities and other costs, as described in Appendix 4., below, shall be reduced by the supporting installation to compensate for the use of school facilities by organizations and/or activities other than the DoDDS.

C1.3.8. <u>Regional Directors</u>.   Individuals employed by the DoDDS who manage several districts and offices in a defined geographical area.

C1.4. FUNCTIONS AND RESPONSIBILITIES

C1.4.1. Under DoD Directive 1342.6 (reference (a)), the Director, DoDDS, shall:

C1.4.1.1. Organize, manage, fund, direct, and supervise the complete operation of the DoDDS and issue such policies, guidance, and regulations, as necessary, to carry out the assigned mission.

C1.4.1.2. Enter into agreements with the Military Departments, other U.S. Government entities, or private parties as required for the effective performance of the DoDDS program.

C1.4.1.3. Establish subordinate offices necessary to fulfill the assigned mission.

C1.4.1.4. Assist the Assistant Secretary of Defense (Economic Security) in the development and justification of school construction, modification, and/or repair projects included in annual military construction (MILCON) programs.

C1.4.1.5. Authorize and fund the procurement of all administrative and instructional supplies, services and equipment necessary to carry out the mission of the DoDDS.

C1.4.2. Each Secretary of the Military Departments shall:

C1.4.2.1. Ensure that subordinate activities provide logistic and administrative support to DoDDS activities, as prescribed in DoD Instruction 4000.19 (reference (c)) and this Manual. That is to include categories of support such as "contracting services," "maintaining equipment," and "disposing of property" as addressed in Chapter 4., below.

C1.4.2.2. Establish logistic support policies and help resolve support problems that may arise.

C1.4.2.3. Notify the Director, DoDDS, of expected changes in comand personnel support levels or support provided (e.g., medically related services) that shall affect the operation of any school.

C1.4.2.4. Act as construction agent for the DoDDS MILCON Program. Engineering support shall include, as a minimum, design and contract services.

C1.4.2.5. Comply with the responsibilities enumerated in DoD Directive 1015.5 (reference (d)) for the Student Meal Program.

C1.4.2.6. Fund second-destination transportation costs for DoDDS supplies and equipment (except for the Panama/Islands Region) in designated theaters.

C1.4.3. The Installation Commanders shall:

C1.4.3.1. Provide logistic and administrative support to local DoDDS activities, in accordance with this Manual, cost ceilings established by the DoDDS regional director and the applicable Interservice Support Agreement(s) (ISAs). That support includes all necessary contract procurement support needed by the DoDDS to ensure the enrollment of children in non-DoDDS schools, to transport children, and to obtain contracted supplies and services.

C1.4.3.2. Provide support engineering services, as in Chapter 5., below, when the construction of new school facilities or maintenance, repair, and O&M-funded minor construction projects are proposed.

C1.4.3.3. Provide services and/or equipment required, within mission constraints. Those services and/or equipment shall be provided at the same level as to all other users to include the installation's organizational units.

C1.4.3.4. Ensure that community use of the school facilities and/or equipment does not hinder, jeopardize, or interfere with the facility's primary educational purpose. School equipment and supplies must be conserved for dependents education. The following guidelines shall apply on the use of school facilities for purposes other than dependents education:

C1.4.3.4.1. Any command-sanctioned activity or organization wishing to use any of the school facilities and/or equipment, on a temporary or recurring basis, shall submit a written request to the installation commander. The request must specify the time, frequency, space, and equipment requirements by the activity or organization.

C1.4.3.4.2. Before granting approval, the installation commander shall, after determining that no other adequate base facilities are available, forward the request to the school principal for concurrence. The principal may approve or disapprove requests to use the school facilities and/or equipment. Before the use of equipment, the organization sponsor must enter into an agreement with the installation commander to ensure timely and effective repair or replacement of equipment lost, damaged, or destroyed at no cost to the DoDDS. The base legal office shall review the agreement and a copy of the agreement shall be provided to the school principal.

C1.4.3.4.3. The activity sponsor shall ensure that the rooms used are left in the same condition as found and that the windows and doors are secured before departing. Failure on the part of an activity sponsor to ensure building cleanliness and security may result in forfeiture of the privilege to use the school.

C1.4.3.5. Provide copies of school leases to the school principal and the DoDDS regional office.

C1.4.3.6. Encourage all eligible dependents who have not comp leted high school to enroll in a DoDDS approved education program. If a DoDDS program is unsuitable to the parents, the installation commander shall encourage the parents to enroll their dependents in an alternate program.

C1.4.3.7. Inform the pertinent District Superintendent's Office of the names and duty locations of all known incoming school age dependents and ensure that the sponsors of such dependents are informed about school locations, commuting areas, and school sponsored meetings to introduce sponsors to school programs.

C1.4.3.8. Notify DoD sponsors and take corrective action when advised by the school principals of serious or repeated misbehavior, including truancy and criminal acts by students. Installation commanders agree to consider arrangements to permit the child to attend school even though action is taken to otherwise bar them from accessing the installation (for other than medical care). The installation commander shall also consider whether command sponsorship should be withdrawn.

C1.4.3.9. Provide cost estimates for reimbursable and direct cite logistic support services specified in the ISAs to the DoDDS regional director. Provide such reimbursable support commensurate with authorized funding and overall installation capability.

C1.4.3.10. Provide civilian personnel services for foreign national (FN) employees in accordance with applicable law, treaty, and regulation.

C1.4.3.11. Provide complete custodial service to school facilities (including leased DoDDS facilities, warehouses, and repair facilities) on a reimbursable or direct-cite basis. The DoDDS representative must be a primary contributor to the development of the performance work statement to ensure that the DoDDS requirements are met.

C1.4.3.12. Provide a dormitory facility and reimbursable food service for dormitory students where a dormitory has been approved by the Director, DoDDS. Repair and rehabilitate all furnishings and equipment, including drycleaning of blankets, draperies, and similar items through an ISA.   The funding policy in Chapter 3., below, applies.

C1.4.3.13. Appoint a staff member (generally a member with an interest in education) who has demonstrated effectiveness, maturity and leadership as a military commissioned officer, an officer-grade civilian, or a senior noncommissioned officer to serve as an installation school's officer.   The school's officer shall function as a liaison between the school principal(s) and the Military Department installation staff, but shall not be assigned responsibility for any aspect of operating the school(s). Preferably the school's officer should be physically located in the headquarters area rather than in the school.

C1.4.3.14. Grant Status of Forces Agreement status to dependents who are enrolled in the DoDDS under DoD Directive 1342.13 (reference (e)) when the enrollment provides a benefit not contemplated by Military Department regulations about command sponsorship.

C1.4.3.15. Support the various types of parent-teacher-student organizations that provide liaison, volunteer support, or financial assistance to the school or school activities.   Ensure that activities sponsored by local organizations or individuals that involve student participation do not conflict with the regular school program.

C1.4.3.16. Ensure that school facilities meet all applicable facility fire, physical security, safety, sanitation, and enviroranental protection requirements. Assign qualified personnel to perform the following inspections of school facilities:

C1.4.3.16.1. Before the start of the school year (SY), an inspection by qualified facility, physical security, safety, sanitation, bioenvironmental, and fire protection specialists to identify all facilities deficiencies and requirements and their relative priority for repair or maintenance.

C1.4.3.16.2. In January, an inspection by qualified facility, physical security, safety, sanitation, bioenvironmental, and fire protection specialists to identify all facilities deficiencies and requirements and their relative priority for accomplishment.   The second physical security inspection in January is not required for those schools located on military installations protected by positive entry control procedures.

C1.4.3.16.2.1. The inspection report shall be the basis for maintenance and repair work to be accomplished during the summer recess.

C1.4.3.16.2.2. The facilities engineer shall develop projects or program actions to eliminate all other identified deficiencies.

C1.4.3.17. Provide billeting (or instead of, a certificate of non-availability) in adequate Government-furnished quarters for eligible DoDDS employees. DoDDS employees shall be given equal consideration on the basis of comparable-grade military personnel for Government quarters assignments and furnishings in accordance with the regulations of the host Military Department, unless otherwise prescribed in an applicable collective bargaining agreement.

C1.4.3.18. Ensure that postal service for personal, as well as official, mail is provided in accordance with DoD postal regulations to include the pickup and sorting of mail for the DoDDS. Mailing costs for official mail shall be computed for each school in accordance with DoD 4525.8-M (reference (f)).

C1.4.3.19. Provide security for school facilities. Unusual, unique, or extraordinary security requirements for the sole benefit of the DoDDS, which are of a recurring nature and exceed the installation commander's capabilities are reimbursable, but must first be approved by the DoDDS regional director. School administrators should be informed of the community antiterrorism and crime prevention programs.

C1.4.3.20. Ensure that the personal effects of deceased DoDDS personnel, which are under U.S. Government control, are promptly secured and disposed of, in accordance with applicable Military Department directives.

C1.4.3.21. In coordination with the school principal, close school, as necessary, in emergency conditions (for example, fire, bomb threats, or military actions) or when facility deficiencies or inclement weather endanger the health and safety of students and school personnel.

C1.4.3.22. Provide student transportation services using the most cost-effective (to the U.S. Government) mode for daily commuting and dormitory transportation as well as curricular and co-curricular activity travel. Comply with DoD 4500.36-R, Chapter 6 (reference (g)).

C1.4.3.23. Provide Government vehicles with or without drivers to transport DoDDS personnel and material on "official business" (reference (g)).

"Domicile-to-duty" transportation is not authorized. Trucks or special purpose vehicles may be assigned on a reimbursable basis to meet recurring logistic requirements.

C1.4.3.24. Refer parents, guardians, or sponsors with problems about DoDDS academic operations to the school principal.

C1.4.3.25. Provide medical treatment in overseas areas, in accordance with Military Department regulations for DoDDS personnel and DoD dependent students. Provide medically related services to DoD dependent handicapped students in accordance with DoD Instruction 1010.13 (reference (h)) on the same priority as is accorded to active duty members. Provide medical support for interscholastic athletic contests (see Chapter 2., Section C2.5., below).

C1.4.3.26. Provide accounting and finance services to include civilian payroll services, processing, and payment of travel claims, and cashier services, on a recurring and permanent basis.

C1.4.3.27. Comply with the responsibilities of DoD Directive 1015.5 (reference (d)) for the DoD Student Meal Program.

C1.4.4. The DoDDS Regional Directors shall:

C1.4.4.1. Negotiate, implement, review, and monitor administrative and logistic support provided to dependents schools by installation commanders. Responsibility for those functions may be delegated to the district superintendent's office.

C1.4.4.2. Ensure, in coordination with local military officials, that antiterrorism emergency plans are established to respond to increased terrorist threat conditions.

C1.4.4.3. With the prior approval of the Director, DoDDS, establish and disestablish dependents schools and dormitories, in coordination with the installation commanders concerned. Establish a summer school with the prior approval of the Director, DoDDS.

C1.4.4.4. Program, budget, and fund all appropriated fund costs of the dependents education system, investment items not in MILCON accounts, school minor construction projects less than 300,000 dollars, and reimbursable logistic support costs. Perform statistical analyses of the above costs to ensure the most economical use of resources. Prepare estimates for annual budgets based on inputs received from principals and other DoDDS administrators and from operations budget submissions from installation commanders.

C1.4.4.5. Use Military Inter-Departmental Purchase Requests (MIPRs) to establish fund targets and expense authorizations for administrative and logistic support. Approve the fiscal arrangements of support agreements. Approval authority may be delegated to the district superintendent or a principal. Ensure that obligation and commitment documents are processed in accordance with approved accounting procedures.

C1.4.4.6. Reimburse the providing activity for identifiable reimbursable logistic and administrative support costs, in accordance with the negotiated ISAs and this Manual.

C1.4.4.7. Certify the adequacy and suitability of the educational program provided to DoD-sponsored students by non-DoD overseas schools through periodic visits and reviews.

C1.4.4.8. Program, budget, fund (through appropriations or by reimbursement), and place all authorized space-required, tuition-free students and specified tuition-paying students seeking to enroll in the DoDDS, non-DoDDS schools, or correspondence courses.

C1.4.4.9. Prepare enrollment reports and forecasts in coordination with the Military Services and other organizations as necessary.

C1.4.4.10. When authorized by the Director, DoDDS, arrange for the leasing of a facility.

C1.4.4.11. When approved by the Director, DoDDS, establish advisory committees and employ part-time advisors.

C1.4.4.12. Contract for supplies, equipment, and services required for mission accomplishment with the approval of the Director, DoDDS. Contract actions shall be administered through the DoDDS or military procurement office, in accordance with paragraph C1.4.3.1., above, or, when consistent with the Federal Acquisition Regulations, through another DoD or other U.S. Government activity.

C1.4.4.13. Oversee and manage the implementation of this Manual, to include, where consistent with law and regulation, the authorization of reasonable exceptions to this Manual that are necessary to ensure the orderly administration of the DoDDS mission.

C1.4.4.14. Direct that a DoDDS representative be included on any Family Advocacy Committee or Family Advocacy Case Management Team activity involving DoDDS employees in their capacity as an employee, or as deemed appropriate by the school principal or Family Advocacy program manager or officer.

C1.4.5. The <u>District Superintendents</u> shall:

C1.4.5.1. Maintain effective liaison with representatives of the Military Department command(s).

C1.4.5.2. Negotiate for, implement, and monitor, when required and within the constraints imposed by the DoDDS regional director, all logistic and administrative support furnished by host Military Department installations (for example, custodial services) to the district schools and the district office. Inform command officials of deficiencies and certify to the regional office that adequate reimbursable administrative and logistic support has been provided.

C1.4.6. The <u>School Principals</u> shall:

C1.4.6.1. Consider the advice of the community, including, for example, the installation commander, the local advisory committees, parent groups, and the Parent Teacher Student Association when planning the operation of the school.

C1.4.6.2. Establish and coordinate emergency disaster plans with local installation commanders.

C1.4.6.3. Identify and submit administrative and logistic support requirements to the military Department supporting installation through lead principals, district superintendents, or DoDDS regional directors, as applicable.

C1.4.6.4. Participate with appropriate Department of Defense accounting and finance offices and MIPR acceptors, in periodic reviews of unliquidated obligations and fiscal year (FY) end closures of assigned funds.

C1.4.6.5. Ensure that accurate requirements for maintenance, repair, alteration, and minor construction projects are submitted to the activity in a proper and timely manner. Those requests shall be coordinated with the activity supporting the school. Ensure that all school equipment requiring maintenance is reported on correctly prepared density listings to the supporting maintenance activity for the type of equipment requiring repair. Ensure that excess property is reported as required and that hazardous wastes are disposed of in accordance with installation guidelines and host nation laws and regulations. School administrators should seek the advice of the safety officer before disposal of hazardous wastes.

C1.4.6.6. Be responsible for enrolling students and for:

C1.4.6.6.1. Determining student eligibility, in accordance with DoD Directive 1342.13 (reference (e)). Eligibility questions should be referred to the regional office or the DoDDS General Counsel when necessary.

C1.4.6.6.2. Collecting tuition, depositing funds, and assisting with the processing of debt collection actions.

C1.4.6.6.3. Establishing school hours.

C1.4.6.7. Ensure that appropriate disciplinary measures are initiated when a child's behavior is disruptive to the school environment or threatens the safety or welfare of other students or staff. Ensure that proper due process is accorded, especially in suspension and expulsion matters. Inform installation commanders of serious or repeated misbehavior, including chronic school truancy and criminal acts of students. With respect to children with disabilities, the requirements of DoD Instruction 1342.12 (reference (i)), shall apply.

C1.4.6.8. Coordinate with the installation commander to ensure that school facilities are inspected as in paragraph C1.4.3.17., above.

C1.4.6.9. Ensure that fire exit drills are conducted once a week for the first 4 weeks of a new SY and at least 6 additional fire exit drills are conducted during the balance of the SY.

C1.4.6.10. In coordination with the installation commander, approve or disapprove requests for the use of school facilities, equipment, and grounds by nonschool activities.

C1.4.6.11. Develop school evacuation procedures in coordination with the Military Department officials. School staff shall be responsible for students who are on school grounds or in alternate facilities until the emergency is over or students are sent home. Incidents that may require delayed opening or early closure of a school are generally classified as "urgent safety or security" problems such as severe weather, loss of heating, or anticipated civil disturbances, or as "emergencies" such as fire, bomb threats, or military actions.

C1.4.6.11.1. During urgent safety or security problems such as severe weather or failure of a utility service, which adversely affects the instructional program, the local installation commander or designated representative and the principal shall coordinate the school closure. They shall consider the severity of the weather or effect of the utility failure on the instructional program, the availability of distances for students to and from the school and decide whether or not to close the school.

C1.4.6.11.2. During an "emergency," the following procedures shall be used:

C1.4.6.11.2.1. The party (the principal or the installation commander) who first learns of the emergency shall notify the other party, and determine whether or not facilities are to be evacuated. Generally, it is the responsibility of the installation commander to order the evacuation of a facility. If the school principal is unable to contact the installation commander, or if time does not permit the principal to contact the installation commander, the principal may order the evacuation.

C1.4.6.11.2.2. If required, the principal shall evacuate the school and provide for continuance of the educational program primarily through large group instruction in predetermined alternate facilities.

C1.4.6.11.2.3. If the school is closed because of the weather or emergency conditions and the students are sent home, the principal shall request authority from the installation commander to release the teachers from duty. The installation commander's decision should be based on the same criteria used for releasing other civilian employees. The absence of students, in itself, is not a justifiable reason for teacher release.

C1.4.6.11.2.4. The district superintendent and the DoDDS regional director should be notified as soon as possible of action taken.

C1.4.6.12. Ensure that the installation commander is informed of the unavailability of medically related services for a DoD dependent with a valid individualized education program, in accordance with reference (i).

C1.5. ESTABLISHMENT AND/OR DISESTABLISHMENT OF DEPENDENTS SCHOOLS

C1.5.1. <u>General</u>.   The Director, DoDDS, shall establish or disestablish DoD Dependents Schools in consultation with the Military Departments concerned.

C1.5.2. <u>Requirements</u>.   With the prior approval of the Director, DoDDS, DoD Dependents Schools may be established and serviced by the DoDDS regional director when the following general criteria are met:

C1.5.2.1. <u>Establishment</u>

C1.5.2.1.1.   An enrollment of at least 100 space-required dependents is ensured for an elementary school (K through 6 or K through 8), and an enrollment of at least 300 space-required dependents is ensured for a secondary school (7 through 12 or 9 through 12).   K through 12 schools must meet both of the foregoing requirements.   Minimum school enrollment size alone shall not be the sole criterion for determining establishment and disestablishment of DoD Dependents Schools in overseas areas.   The availability of alternative educational opportunities, safety, and hardships shall be given consideration.   Exceptions for establishing schools that do not meet the minimum school enrollment size must have prior approval of the Director, DoDDS.

C1.5.2.1.2.   Adequate facilities for school classrooms including the necessary instructional and ancillary spaces,, installed equipment, grounds development, safety requirements, and support systems in accordance with Appendix 1. are available.

C1.5.2.1.3.   Adequate administrative and logistic support (including medically related services) in accordance with DoD Instruction 1013.13 and DoD Instruction 1342.12 (references (h) and (i)) is available from the designated "supporting Military Department installation" and includes, at a minimum, the categories listed in Appendices 2. and 3., below.

C1.5.2.2. <u>Disestablishment</u>

C1.5.2.2.1.   Unless otherwise determined by the Director, DoDDS, DoD Dependents Schools shall be disestablished and/or closed or not opened when the following criteria apply:

C1.5.2.2.1.1. Number of space-available students exceeds the number of space-required students.

C1.5.2.2.1.2. Additional cost of school operations attributable to space-available students exceeds the amount of tuition collected at that location and retained by the DoDDS.

C1.5.2.2.1.3. The number of space-required students (excluding dependents of school employee sponsors) would be insufficient to warrant operation of a quality school.

C1.5.2.2.2. DoD Dependents Schools may also be disestablished and/or closed or not opened when one or more of the following criteria are met:

C1.5.2.2.2.1. Actual or anticipated school enrollments fall below required levels for school establishment.

C1.5.2.2.2.2. School facilities are inadequate.

C1.5.2.2.2.3. Logistic support including medically related services is not available.

C1.5.2.2.2.4. Changes in school enrollment and student attendance patterns, or availability of new school facilities, require changes in school configuration.

C1.5.3. <u>Procedures</u>

C1.5.3.1. Installation commanders shall begin requests for establishing DoD Dependents Schools and submit them through the chain of command to the DoDDS regional director. Letter requests shall include the following information:

C1.5.3.1.1. The total number of families to be served by the school, both those physically present and those programed to arrive during the current and next 3 SYs.

C1.5.3.1.2. The number of space-required students by grade level. Children with known learning or other disabilities should be noted and listed separately.

C1.5.3.1.3. A description of the facilities for dependents school use with a blueprint or schematic floor plan enclosed. If alteration of facilities is necessary, a preplanning consultation with the DoDDS regional director is required before engineering drawings are made. Those projects must also be reviewed by the commander of the supporting medical treatment facility (MTF) and by a safety officer to ensure compliance with DoD health and safety directives.

C1.5.3.1.4. Description of housing arrangements for teachers, dormitory students, and school administrators.

C1.5.3.1.5. A statement that an installation school's officer has been or shall be appointed for the proposed school.

C1.5.3.1.6. A statement that adequate administrative and logistic support is available from the supporting Military Department installation and includes, at a minimum, the categories listed in Appendices 2. and 3., below.

C1.5.3.2. On receiving the installation commander's request, a representative of the DoDDS regional director shall inspect the plans of the proposed school building. The inspector's report to the DoDDS regional director shall include specific comments about each point in the request and a recommendation.

C1.5.4. Day-Care Facilities. The DoDDS shall not establish or operate day-care facilities. Day-care facilities provide hourly, part-time, and full day child care for minor dependent children.

C1.6. INSPECTOR GENERAL (IG) ACTIVITIES

C1.6.1. The Military Department IGs and their representatives shall accept complaints and requests for assistance at the local level from DoDDS employees. The Military Department IGs or their representatives may informally resolve the complaint or request for assistance. If the complaint or request for assistance requires formal inquiry or investigation of a DoDDS activity, the action shall be forwarded to the DoDDS Internal Review office, or the Office of the IG, Department of Defense (OIG, DoD).

C1.6.2. The Military Department IGs and their representatives shall perform inspections or reviews of DoDDS activities only at the specific request of DoDDS management officials or the IG, DoD.

C1.6.3. DoDDS management officials shall render assistance and access to information necessary for the OIG, DoD, and the Military IGs in their conduct of audits, reviews, inquiries, inspections, and investigations of military activities that support the DoDDS and of DoDDS activities and employees.

C1.7. TRANSPORTATION FOR DORMITORY STUDENTS

C1.7.1. Authorized Services. In locations where a DoDDS high school is not available, students in grades 9 through 12 shall normally be assigned to a DoDDS high school with dormitory facilities.

C1.7.1.1. DoDDS authorizes and will fund and/or reimburse for the following transportation:

C1.7.1.1.1. With a 5-day dormitory program; transportation from residence to the school and/or dormitory in time for the beginning of each school week and return at the completion of the school week.

C1.7.1.1.2. With a 7-day dormitory program:

C1.7.1.1.2.1. Transportation from residence to school and/or dormitory at the beginning of the SY and return at the completion of the SY. Each student is also authorized shipment of 350 pounds (159 kilos) of unaccompanied baggage to and from the dormitory with that travel.

C1.7.1.1.2.2. Round-trip transportation from the school and/or dormitory to the student's residence and return, which usually coincides with the winter (Christmas) recess and the spring (Easter) recess.

C1.7.1.2. Students enrolled in, or proposed for, a special education program are authorized transportation for the provision of medically related services, including evaluations and treatment. DoDDS will fund for travel in conjunction with evaluations requested or required by DoDDS. The respective military community in which the sponsor resides will fund for all other medically related transportation. Refer to DoD Instructions 1342.12 and 1010.13 (references (h) and (i)) for further guidance.

C1.7.2. Services Not Authorized. The DoDDS has neither the responsibility nor the authority to provide the following:

C1.7.2.1. Except as authorized in paragraph C1.7.1.2., above, transportation for medical purposes is the responsibility of the sponsor or of the sponsor's military command.

C1.7.2.2. Transportation required as a result of suspension or expulsion from school or dormitory. Subsection C1.7., through paragraphs C1.7.1.1. and C1.7.1.2.,above, are matters for resolution either by the parent or guardian (for non-DoD students) or by the installation commander (for DoD students). DoDDS transportation responsibility terminates on referral of the situation to either the parent or guardian or supporting installation commander. That policy is consistent with practices followed by schools in the United States.

C1.8. SCHOOL NAMES

Normally, the school shall be named after the city or town where the installation is located, followed by the words "Elementary School" or "High School," as applicable. Schools may be named for honored individuals at the request of the installation commander, endorsed by the theater commander, and forwarded to the DoDDS regional director for decision. Schools named for an honored person shall be followed by the geographic location (for example, the Joshua Barney Elementary School, Gaeta, Italy).

C2. CHAPTER 2

MEDICAL RESPONSIBILITIES AND PROCEDURES

C2.1. GENERAL

The success of the school health program depends on the cooperative efforts of all healthcare delivery components; i.e., home, school, MTFs, and community. Program emphasis is on health education, health services, and maintenance of a healthful school environment.

C2.2. DoDDS RESPONSIBILITIES

C2.2.1. School officials shall refer ill or injured children requiring emergency treatment to the supporting MTF. School officials may request ambulance transportation for a student to the supporting MTF.

C2.2.2. When required as part of the individualized education program for a handicapped student, physical and occupational therapy should be provided at the child's school. If space is not available at the school, then physical and occupational therapy services should be provided at a location that best serves the child's needs, as determined by the principal, the installation commander, the parents, and the medical authority. The military medical facility will furnish the necessary transportation of the child between the school and the site of the therapy.

C2.3. PARENT'S, GUARDIAN'S, OR SPONSOR'S RESPONSIBILITIES

C2.3.1. Parents, guardians, or sponsors of children entering school for the first time (kindergarten or first grade) shall be requested to make an appointment before the first day in school for their child's complete health appraisal by the MTF responsible for primary medical care. Parents, guardians, or sponsors shall maintain student immunizations in accordance with DoD Instruction 6205.1 (reference (j)). Parents, guardians, or sponsors must secure the necessary medical certification on DS Form 122, "DoDDS Certification of Immunization," within 10 working days of enrolling their students. Failure to present certification may result in the disenrollment of the child until the certification is provided. All schools shall comply with the total immunization program. Immunization shall be a condition of attendance in the DoDDS system.

C2.3.2. When a student is registered in school, parents, guardians, or sponsors shall be asked to report any known condition that requires, or may require, special medical or educational consideration. That information shall be recorded in the student's health or educational record.

C2.3.3. School health services (i.e., immunizations and sports physicals) are identical for all students, including those who pay tuition. Adjunct services that provide definitive medical care to an individual outside the school environment can only be given, at U.S. Government expense, to those eligible for such care. Parents, guardians, or sponsors, who are not authorized DoD medical care, must make other arrangements for their children. When emergency care is needed to prevent loss of life or limb, and to prevent undue suffering, medical care shall be provided. The MTF providing the emergency treatment shall bill the non-DoD parent, guardian, or sponsor for that service after the fact.

C2.4. SUPPORTING MILITARY INSTALLATION'S RESPONSIBILITIES

C2.4.1. Supporting Military Department installation medical officers shall support school health programs, in accordance with applicable Military Service Departmental regulations. The local MTF shall provide diagnoses, medical treatment, follow-up and necessary needs described in this Manual for eligible students. Each Exceptional Family Member Program Clinic must evaluate all students referred from the DoDDS Case Study Committee under special education eligibility and medically related health determinations. The local facility shall provide necessary emergency care, medical supplies sufficient to meet the student needs described in this Manual and all medically related services required for a DoDDS student to benefit from a special education program.

C2.4.2. Other Agencies, such as the Army Community Service, the Child Advocacy Board, the American Red Cross, the community drug and alcohol programs, and the community health nurse are available to serve as resources in support of the school health program.

C2.4.3. Each Exceptional Family Member Program Clinic, or designated MTF, must evaluate students referred from the DoDDS Case Study Committee pursuant to special education eligibility and medically related service determinations and provide all medically related services required to benefit from a special education program.

CHAPTER 2

C2.5. INTERSCHOLASTIC ATHLETIC PROGRAM

C2.5.1. Physical Examinations. Each student wishing to participate in an interscholastic sport must present to school officials a valid physical examination form signed by a healthcare provider, stating that the candidate is medically qualified to participate in the designated sport(s). Local installation commanders, supporting medical personnel, and school personnel may arrange, on an ad hoc basis, for organized group examinations to be conducted in the schools, the community centers, or the MTFs. Non-DoD dependent students who arrange for physical examinations with their own private physicians as opposed to participation in group examinations through the MTFs are responsible for payment of associated fees. Arrangements for reimbursing for individual student costs incurred, if any, shall be part of the terms agreed to during negotiation.

C2.5.2. Athletic Contests. The host school shall arrange with the local MTF for adequate medical support, as determined by the senior medical officer, for interscholastic athletic contests when requested by school officials. The local MTF shall provide emergency medical service during contact sports. If emergency medical support cannot be provided for contact sports, the games shall be canceled.

C3. CHAPTER 3

FINANCIAL ADMINISTRATION

C3.1. POLICY

C3.1.1. The DoDDS shall program, prioritize, and budget for all requirements. That includes O&M, Procurement, and MILCON appropriations. MILCON basic project specifications shall include all items chargeable to military construction accounts. The DoDDS provides funds from direct funding and tuition receipts.

C3.1.2. Support agreements between the DoDDS and the Military Departments shall be accomplished, in accordance with the policies in DoD Instruction 4000.19 (reference (c)). Appendix 2., below, is a list of support categories that military installations shall furnish to the DoDDS on a reimbursable basis, in accordance with DoD standards, agreements reached between the Military Department installations and the DoDDS and the Military Departments's policies and procedures, in that order. Appendix 3., below, lists administrative and logistic support which Military Department installations shall furnish to the DoDDS on a nonreimbursable basis. The DoDDS shall not be billed for the following:

C3.1.2.1. The costs for supervisors and other indirect cost personnel, unless a unit is established solely to serve the DoDDS; in which case, only the costs of the sole support unit are chargeable to the DoDDS, or

C3.1.2.2. Military personnel.

C3.1.3. When providing reimbursable services to the DoDDS under a support agreement, the installation commander may rely on in-house resources or contracted services, and shall employ whichever is most cost-effective to the U.S. Government.

C3.1.4. The installation commanders are responsible for providing civilian personnel administration for foreign national employees, in accordance with law, treaty, and regulation on a reimbursable basis, as specified in servicing agreements negotiated at the installation level.

C3.1.5. The Military Departments may provide nonappropriated funds for school activities not chargeable to appropriated funds.

C3.1.6. When the school facilities are used by organizations and/or activities other than the DoDDS, the costs of utilities, custodial services, refuse collection, facility leases, and other basic engineering support shall be reduced by the applicable OUF (Chapter 1., subsection C1.3.7., above).   The standard OUF is established at 20 percent and shall be documented in a memorandum of understanding between the region and the major military theater commands to cover the ISAs negotiated with installations in that command.   The OUF shall not be negotiated lower than the major military theater command level unless both the respective DoDDS regional director and the supporting military theater command agree.   Decisions to negotiate the OUF at lower levels shall be the exception rather than the rule and shall be made on a case by case basis by the regional director.   When the use of the 20-percent factor would clearly be inequitable to either the major theater commands or the DoDDS, a revised factor may be renegotiated.   The standard factor of 20 percent shall be used to reduce the cost of services billed to the DoDDS (see Appendix 4., below) until another factor is renegotiated.   The party disputing the 20-percent factor (either the DoDDS or the military theater command) must provide supporting documentation to justify a different factor.   In cases where the OUF is recomputed, it shall be calculated by prorating each and every user's share of the facility at each and every location. Factors making up the calculation must include the actual square footage used increased by a factor of 40 percent, to account for common-use areas (i.e., halls, locker rooms, and restrooms, etc.).   When support categories are provided by contract performance, both the DoDDS and the supporting Military Service installation's funds shall be cited for 80 percent and 20 percent respectively, or the renegotiated rate. Once negotiated, the OUF shall be reviewed triennially to coincide with the ISA review, or at the request of either party.   The OUF shall not be recomputed more frequently than every 12th month and when recomputed shall not be retroactively applied by either party.

C3.2. BUDGETING

C3.2.1. Performing installations shall provide budget estimates for reimbursable administrative and logistic support, in accordance with guidance issued by the DoDDS regional directors.   Budget estimates shall include cost, workload, and other information needed to prepare budget documents on a timely basis.

C3.2.2. Supplier activities that have provided support without charge, but decide to identify costs and seek reimbursement, must allow sufficient lead time for the DoDDS to evaluate requests and to budget for requirements through the planning process.   Those issues shall be resolved at the regional level.

C3.2.3. Military installation commanders that provide support services must ensure that obligations and billings do not exceed funding provided by the MIPR and that all services specified in the agreement are delivered, and that funds in excess of services delivered are returned. DoDDS personnel must monitor obligations and billings to ensure that services requested are in fact received and billed. Performing activities must absorb any excess costs. Adjustments between the MIPR cost categories may be made if the DoDDS agrees, total funding is not exceeded, facility maintenance floors are met, and requested services are provided.

C3.3. FUNDING PROCEDURES

C3.3.1. The DD Form 1144, "Interservice Support Agreement (ISA)," shall be used to establish supplier and/or receiver relationships. The ISAs must show cost estimates for all related costs of specific categories of support regardless of whether the support is provided on a reimbursable or direct cite basis. The ISAs are not funding documents.

C3.3.2. The DoDDS shall prepare a DD Form 448, MIPR, in accordance with Subpart 253.208-1 of the DFARS (reference (k)), to order services, in accordance with the ISA. DoDDS regional offices, district offices, or schools may prepare the MIPRS. The MIPRs shall be issued to the commanding officer, or designee, of the installation performing the services. Amounts specified in the MIPRs shall reflect official DoD-budgeted foreign currency exchange rates.

C3.3.3. In accordance with Subpart 253-208-2 of the DFARS, commanding officers, or designee, of the support installations shall return the DD Forms 448-2, "Acceptance of MIPR," to the DoDDS (the issuing activity). Acceptances shall be provided as soon as practicable, but not later than 15 days after receipt of the DD Form 448. At year end, acceptances should be processed and returned within 24 hours.

C3.3.4. Military Department installations shall accept MIPRs on a reimbursable basis unless the DoDDS has agreed that direct-cite funding is more appropriate. For example, fixed-price contracts negotiated exclusively for the DoDDS are usually direct cite. Copies of direct-cite contracts shall be forwarded to the school principal and the DoDDS regional office expeditiously, but no later than 15 days from contract award date.

C3.3.5. The DoDDS shall normally issue one MIPR for each ISA to simplify processing and to reduce administrative costs. The DoDDS may issue separate MIPRs for each category of support.   In either case, the MIPRs must specify the specific support categories and the ISA number.

C3.3.6. Supporting Military Department installations shall bill DoDDS monthly (see DoD 4000.25-7-M, reference (l)) for services provided in accordance with the ISAS.   Billing documents shall be SF 1080, "Voucher for Transfers between Appropriations and/or Funds," or Military Service equivalents.   Along with sufficient supporting documentation, billings shall be submitted according to local procedures specified in the MIPR and the ISA.

C3.3.7. In accordance with Subpart 253.208-2 of the DFARS (reference (k)), all billing, shipping, contractual, and related documentation that installations provide to the DoDDS shall identify the MIPRS, quantities, and costs.   Specifically, supporting documentation shall include the following:

C3.3.7.1. Reference to the MIPR number being billed.

C3.3.7.2. The type of service being billed.

C3.3.7.3. Application of the OUF.

C3.3.7.4. The unit cost and units utilized in deriving current billing.

C3.3.7.5. Current and prior cumulative amounts billed.   Erroneous charges discovered after billing shall be corrected on subsequent bills.

C3.4. ACCOUNTING

C3.4.1. For the DoDDS, the DD Form 448 is the basis for a commitment of funds.   When accepted on a reimbursable basis, the DD Form 448-2 creates an obligation.   Direct-cite MIPRs remain as commitments until evidence of the contract award is received at a DoDDS accounting office.

C3.4.2. For performing Military Department installations, acceptance of a reimbursable MIPR is an unfilled customer order received.

CHAPTER 3

C4. CHAPTER 4

MATERIEL MANAGEMENT

C4.1. PURPOSE

This Chapter prescribes the policies that apply to the DoDDS, and its supporting Military Department installations, for DoDDS materiel support. In carrying out DoDDS mission objectives, each supporting organization should satisfy DoDDS materiel requirements in the most responsive and economical manner.

C4.2. ACQUISITION

The DoDDS is authorized to acquire supplies and equipment necessary to accomplish its mission, in accordance with the instructions in DoD Directive 1342.6 and the DS Manual 4100.2 (references (a) and (m)), and any additional instructions provided by its Headquarters and/or regional offices. The DoDDS determines its own requirements for material. Each DoDDS activity is authorized to submit requirements to a local supporting procurement activity for procurement from local sources and/or those sources in the United States available to the procurement activity, in accordance with the FAR and the DFARS (references (n) and (k)). DoDDS activities shall comply with the submission format required by the supporting contracting activity, timeframes for submission, and other requirements for the procurement function. However, procurements to purchase DoDDS requirements do not require Military Department approvals of purchases or leases of copiers, computers, word processors, and other items that may be controlled for military customers by various functional activities in the military command structure. It is the DoDDS responsibility to comply with restrictions imposed by the OSD, the office of Management and Budget, and the General Services Administration. It is also the DoDDS responsibility to obtain approvals from those authorities, as required, for proposed acquisitions. Authority to approve procurement of Federal information processsing systems, including word processors, is centrally controlled at the DoD Office of Dependents Education. Authority to approve procurement of accountable property rests with the accountable officer at each DoDDS regional office. Authority to approve procurement of expendable and durable items rests with the cognizant DoDDS administrator.

C4.3. ACCOUNTING FOR DoDDS SCHOOL MATERIEL

DoDDS nonexpendable material shall be properly secured and accounted for through the DoDDS property accountability program. Nonexpendable items procured by the supporting Military Department installation for the DoDDS shall be picked up on DoDDS records. The Military Department installation retains accountability only for nonexpendable items on loan to the DoDDS, cafeteria (food service) equipment, and permanently installed equipment in DoDDS facilities.

C4.4. EQUIPMENT MAINTENANCE

Principals and administrators shall ensure that equipment is properly maintained and available for use either in the instructional program or in support of it. Generally, after expiration of any manufacturer's warranties, the Military Department maintenance and repair facility shall perform equipment maintenance modification, repair, and servicing, subject to reimbursement in accordance with the terms of the applicable ISA. When Military Department facilities are unable to perform those services, DoDDS personnel shall secure the repair and maintenance services through the supporting contracting office on a reimbursable basis. Difficulties encountered in obtaining maintenance support shall be reported, through support channels, to the district superintendent and/or the local installation commander.

C5. CHAPTER 5

DoDDS FACILITIES PROGRAMS

C5.1. PURPOSE

This Chapter establishes the policies and procedures between the DoDDS and the Military Departments for school facility maintenance, repair, and minor construction; construction of new school facilities under the MILCON program; leasing of real property facilities; interim or temporary facilities; and facility utilization.

C5.2. POLICY

Although the DoDDS has the responsibility for programing, budgeting, and financing school facility requirements, the Military Departments provide for facility safety, security, environmental compliance, and condition inspections; maintenance and repair; and design and construction contracting services. To properly program DoDDS facilities projects, major military Department commands have an obligation to provide the cognizant DoDDS regional directors with troop stationing and related student population projections consistent with the approved Future Years Defense Program. Military major commands have a further responsibility to provide timely notification of mission changes, or other factors, which shall affect school populations. This Chapter outlines specific responsibilities for executing the DoDDS facilities programs.

C5.3. RESPONSIBILITIES FOR THE FACILITIES MAINTENANCE, REPAIR, AND MINOR CONSTRUCTION PROGRAMS

C5.3.1. The Director, DoDDS, shall:

C5.3.1.1. Monitor accountability, documentation, and cost control.

C5.3.1.2. Distribute funding authority to the DoDDS regional directors, based on available funds and requirements included in the annual regional budget submission.

C5.3.1.3. Delegate limited project approval authority to the individual DoDDS regional directors.

C5.3.1.4. Provide or obtain approval for maintenance, repair, and minor construction projects that exceed the approval authority of the DoDDS regional directors.

C5.3.2. The DoDDS regional directors shall:

C5.3.2.1. Maintain a 5-year maintenance, repair, and minor construction plan (FYMP) for each school in their regions. Grant exceptions to the requirement for that 5-year plan.

C5.3.2.2. Reimburse supporting Military Departments for engineering support in providing maintenance, repair, and minor construction projects approved by school principals within the scope of their authority and the supporting ISA.

C5.3.2.3. Delegate limited project approval authority to the individual principals.

C5.3.2.4. Review individual projects exceeding the approval authority of the school principal.

C5.3.2.5. Develop an annual work plan and maintain records of funded and unfunded projects. Those records shall include project scope of work, engineering approval documentation, and copies of funding documents issued to the servicing military engineers.

C5.3.2.6. Inform school principals and supporting Military Department engineers of project funding status, program changes, cancelation of requirements, or changes in project scope.

C5.3.2.7. Have authority to fund individual projects up to the following limits:

C5.3.2.7.1. Five hundred thousand dollars for any maintenance and/or repair project.

C5.3.2.7.2. Three hundred thousand dollars for minor construction. Individual projects in excess of those amounts shall be documented on a DD Form 1391, "DoDDS Military Construction Project Data," and shall be submitted through channels to the Director, DoDDS, for approval.

C5.3.2.8. Provide specialized information as to educational facility-related occupational safety, health, and environmental requirements in proposed maintenance, repair, and minor construction needs.

C5.3.3 The school principal shall:

C5.3.3.1. Develop and maintain a FYMP and an annual work plan, with the supporting Military Department engineers and DoDDS regional officials.

C5.3.3.2. Act as a site representative for the DoDDS on maintenance, repair, and minor construction facilities projects during both the design and construction phases.

C5.3.3.3. Review and approve the scope of work for maintenance, repair., and minor construction projects with the supporting Military Department engineers and DoDDS regional officials.

C5.3.3.4. Provide administrative and funding approval for maintenance, repair, and minor construction projects within the limits of delegated authority.

C5.3.3.5. Prepare and submit work requests for all identified facilities requirements and maintain a record of status of those work requests.

C5.3.3.6. The responsible installation commanders and supporting Military Department engineers or public works officers shall:

C5.3.3.6.1. Provide design and construction services on a reimbursable basis for all requirements identified and approved for funding by the DoDDS.

C5.3.3.6.2. Coordinate with the school principals and the DoDDS regional offices in executing designs and construction projects.

C5.3.3.6.3. Provide design or construction status reports, when requested by the DoDDS regional office or the school principal.

C5.3.3.6.4. Schedule the execution of projects during summer or holiday vacation periods, if possible, to minimize disruption of school activities.

C5.3.3.6.5. Review each proposed construction project to ensure that the project is compatible with the installation master plan and complies with all codes and regulations.

C5.3.3.6.6. Perform ongoing (minimally, annual) inspections of school facilities to identify necessary facility maintenance and repair requirements and present a report outlining a corrective action program for integration into the FYMP.

C5.4. RESPONSIBILITIES FOR THE MILCON PROGRAM

C5.4.1. The Director, DoDDS, shall:

C5.4.1.1. Establish a 5-year MILCON program.

C5.4.1.2. Establish criteria to identify, justify, and prioritize MILCON requirements.

C5.4.1.3. Budget and distribute funds for design and construction of MILCON projects.

C5.4.1.4. Provide standard design criteria (educational specifications) for projects.

C5.4.1.5. Provide current cost data from the OSD to regional personnel for the timely development of project documents for inclusion in the 5-year MILCON programs.

C5.4.2. The DoDDS regional directors shall:

C5.4.2.1. Identify MILCON project requirements.

C5.4.2.2. Complete project documentation to include DD Forms 1390, 1391 and 1391c, "Military Construction," and provide supplemental project data to the Office of Dependents Education. Cost estimates shall be based on regional Military Department engineers current building costs rather than unit costs and area cost factors provided for specific program years by the OSD.

C5.4.2.3. Prepare any supplemental design criteria (educational specifications) for each project.

C5.4.2.4. Review all phases of project design with the military design and construction agents and ensure that a qualified DoDDS representative with delegated authority attends all design meetings.

C5.4.2.5. Exercise final approval authority over all functional requirements of the facility design.

C5.4.2.6. Validate proposed user-requested change orders during the construction phase before the design and construction agent submits such changes for approval and funding by the Director, DoDDS.

C5.4.3. The responsible installation commanders and Military Department engineers or public works officers shall:

C5.4.3.1. Provide dedicated construction sites of adequate size and location that minimize student transportation costs and that are, in all aspects, safe and functionally suitable and environmentally safe for the conduct of an educational program.

C5.4.3.2. Certify in writing that proposed sites are legally available and that the necessary host-nation approvals have been obtained and documented before beginning project design.

C5.4.3.3. Provide required supporting facilities at the proposed site to include utilities, roads, adequate security, and communications, in accordance with DoD Directive 7150.5 (reference (o)).

C5.4.3.4. Provide complete engineering and technical reviews of all phases of project design and coordinate comments with DoDDS functional reviews to ensure that the desired quality product is obtained.

C5.4.3.5. Ensure that qualified personnel attend all design review meetings.

C5.4.4. MILCON requirements shall be programed, in accordance with DoD Instruction 7040.4 (reference (p)).

C5.5. RESPONSIBILITIES FOR LEASE OF EXISTING REAL PROPERTY FACILITIES

C5.5.1. The Director, DoDDS, shall:

C5.5.1.1. Establish guidelines to determine a method of comparing and/or evaluating leased DoD-operated schools and privately operated tuition-supported schools.

C5.5.1.2. Provide detailed requirements for leased school facilities requirements to the responsible installation commanders or supporting Military Department engineers.

C5.5.1.3. Review and approve proposed lease agreements, and renewals, thereof.

C5.5.1.4. Reimburse installation commanders for lease costs less the applicable OUF, if any.

C5.5.1.5. Approve DoDDS-funded facility maintenance and repair projects beyond the DoDDS regional director's level of authority.

C5.5.2. The responsible installation commanders and Military Department engineers or public works officers shall:

C5.5.2.1. Develop specific facility requirements for submission to the responsible U.S. military real estate Agency.

C5.5.2.2. Participate in all lease negotiations as required by the responsible U.S. military real estate Agency and ensure that all lease agreements include a statement that the Government reserves the right to inspect and accept and/or reject lessor- accomplished work done under the terms and conditions of the lease.

C5.5.2.3. Obtain administrative approval from the DoDDS regional director for maintenance, repair, or construction projects for lease facilities.

C5.6. RESPONSIBILITIES FOR INTERIM OR TEMPORARY FACILITIES

C5.6.1. Interim or temporary facilities may be required for DoDDS activities until such time as the Director, DoDDS, can budget for and complete new school construction under MILCON appropriations allocated for DoDDS projects. Those requirements may result from events such as curriculum expansion, student enrollment growth, or changes in military mission or restationing actions. The use of relocatable buildings to meet interim or temporary requirements is governed by DoD Instruction 4165.56 (reference (q)).

C5.6.2. On the request for additional space by the school principal, installation commanders shall first determine if adequate school facilities can be provided from existing installation resources before leasing or purchasing additional facilities. If so, the installation commander shall provide the facilities for school purposes. If not, the installation commander shall provide a written certification to that effect to the Director, DoDDS, through the DoDDS regional director.

C5.6.2.1. Curriculum Expansion and/or Student Enrollment Growth. When interim or temporary facility requirements result from curriculum expansion or student enrollment growth unrelated to military mission or restationing action, the Director, DoDDS, shall provide funding authority to DoDDS regional directors for newly constructed or leased facilities to meet the requirements.

C5.6.2.2. Military Mission or Restationing Actions. When interim or temporary facility requirements result from military mission or restationing actions, the Military Department shall provide funding for educational facilities until the Director, DoDDS, can obtain funding for the newly established requirement. On notification, the Director, DoDDS, shall program, within established budgetary timeframes, to assume funding for the interim facilities requirement.

C5.7. FACILITY UTILIZATION

The DoDDS shall utilize any facility constructed with MILCON funds to support the requirements of the dependents schools program, in accordance with DoD Directive 7150.5 (reference (o)).

CHAPTER 5

AP1. APPENDIX 1

COMPLETE SCHOOL FACILITY

The following items, as specified by the DoDDS regional director, constitute a complete and adequate facility:

AP1.1. NECESSARY INSTRUCTIONAL AND ANCILLARY SPACES

The number and kinds of classrooms and ancillary spaces shall be determined by the DoDDS regional director based on projected enrollments, grade structure, the program and services to be offered, and the expected staffing level.

AP1.2. INSTALLED EQUIPMENT

All items of installed furnishings, fixtures, and equipment that are authorized for funding under the MILCON account shall be included in new construction and are constituent parts of a complete and adequate facility. Such installed items include, but are not limited to the following:

Acoustical tile	Drinking fountains	Playground Equipment
ADP Circuits	Electrical scoreboards	Shelving (built-in)
Alarm Systems	Electrical fixtures	Shower fixtures
Blackout curtains	Exhaust hoods	Sinks
Bleachers	Fans	Stage hardware
Bulletin boards	Fire Detection equipment	Stage lighting
Cabinets	Food Service equipment (built-in	Student lockers
Carpet		Television antenna and/or conduit
Chalkboards	Gas fixtures	
Clock and Bell System Intercoms	Gymnasium (installed equipment)	Vault (secondary systems schools)
Coat racks	Laboratory experiment stations	Venetian blinds
Compressed air		Vinyl tile
Counters	Latrine fixtures	Wardrobes
Cupboards	Light fixtures	
Curtain hardware	Map Rails	

APPENDIX 1

AP1.3. GROUNDS DEVELOPMENT

Sitings of proposed construction, whether an addition or a complete new facility, are to be in accordance with the installation's master plan.   Besides the master plan, many bases also have base exterior architectural plans or similar documents to guide the detailed development of exteriors and sites of projects.   In support of the school program, outside areas shall be developed to include landscaping, access, parking, bus loading, paved playground and courts, playing fields, bleachers, installed equipment, standards, benches, fencing, lighting, and signage.   In high-terrorist threat areas, projects shall be designed and sited to mitigate terrorist activities.

AP1.4. SAFETY REQUIREMENTS

New facilities must meet all fire, safety, and environmental protection criteria for dependents schools.   All systems and equipment necessary to meet regulatory standards must be provided as integral parts of a complete and adequate facility.   Such items include illuminated exits, panic hardware, alarm systems, emergency lighting, smoke-stop doors, and extinguishing systems.   All new schools shall be designed and made accessible to the physically handicapped.

AP1.5. SUPPORT SYSTEMS

All necessary support systems are parts of a complete and adequate facility.   Such systems are comprised of all utilities, to include special provisions for computers, ventilation, air-conditioning, public address, intercom, telephone, clocks, synchronized bells, master lock systems, and other security systems.

AP2. APPENDIX 2

REIMBURSABLE SUPPORT

The installation commander shall provide the following services, as required, and within mission constraints, to the DoDDS on a reimbursable basis. Reimbursable costs shall be computed only on the level of services provided to the DoDDS, in accordance with the procedures cited in Appendix 4., below. The reimbursable support category codes are keyed to the category codes listed in DoD Instruction 4000.19 (reference (c)).

AP2.1. ADMINISTRATIVE SERVICES (B.1.)

AP2.2. ADP and/or AUTOMATION SERVICES (B.3.)

AP2.3. CIVILIAN PERSONNEL SERVICES (B.4.)

That category includes civilian personnel and payroll services.

AP2.4. COMMUNICATION SERVICES (B.6.)

DoDDS requirements under that category of support include the following:

AP2.4.1. Toll Charges

AP2.4.2. Commercial Telephone and Leased Local Lines

AP2.4.3. Commercial Leased Long Lines. (Used predominantly by the DoDDS.)

AP2.5. CUSTODIAL SERVICES (B.9.)

Adjusted by the OUF.

AP2.6. ENGINEERING SUPPORT (B.11.)

Architectural engineering services.

AP2.7. EQUIPMENT OPERATION, MAINTENANCE AND REPAIR (B.12.)

Limited to maintenance of school equipment.

AP2.8. FACILITIES AND REAL PROPERTY SUPPORT (B.14.)

Facilities rental, when financed from O&M appropriations (adjusted by the OUF, if applicable).

AP2.9. FACILITY MAINTENANCE AND REPAIR (B.15.)

AP2.9.1. Cyclical and recurring maintenance and repair of school facilities (adjusted by OUF).   Cyclical maintenance is defined as "that portion of recurring maintenance and repair, that can be scheduled in the future."   Recurring maintenance is defined as it repair or maintenance that can be expected to occur more than once over the life of the facilities."

AP2.9.2. Maintenance of school grounds to include trash removal, grass cutting, and maintenance of playgrounds and athletic fields extending up to the school and/or structure's walls.   Grounds maintenance shall not be prorated by the OUF.

AP2.9.3. Nonrecurring maintenance, repair, or minor construction projects on school facilities.   Funds cannot be diverted by supplier because of fixed allocations for Maintenance and Repair Property Floor.

A2.9.4. Entomology Services

AP2.10. FINANCE AND ACCOUNTING (B.16.)

AP2.11. FOOD SERVICE (B.17.)

AP2.12. HEALTH SERVICES (B.18.)

Inpatient and outpatient care of DoDDS employees and their dependents in the MTFs. Those charges are to be reimbursed by individuals, not from DoDDS-appropriated funds.

AP2.13. LAUNDRY AND DRY CLEANING (B.22.)

That reimbursable category includes dormitory, DoDDS facility, and school laundry and dry cleaning to include curtains and linens. Excluded from that category is the personal laundry and dry cleaning of dependents or DoDDS employees. High schools with Junior Reserve Officer Training Course programs are authorized to have military uniforms laundered and/or dry cleaned at no cost to the DoDDS.

AP2.14. PRINTING AND REPRODUCTION (B.27.)

AP2.15. PURCHASING AND CONTRACTING SERVICES (B.28.)

That category of reimbursable support includes the following:

AP2.15.1. The prorated salary of personnel involved in purchasing and contracting on DoDDS behalf, only when additional work-years of support, over and above that required by the supporting activity to meet its own needs, are required to support the DoDDS. Contract costs include 3 percent (average) for contract administration.

AP2.15.2. Goods (primarily subsistence items) and services purchased for school curriculum requirements, such as for home economics programs.

AP2.16. REFUSE COLLECTION AND DISPOSAL (B.29.)

Reimbursable, adjusted by the OUF. Refuse collection and disposal on behalf of the school lunch program is the responsibility of the host Military Department installation.

AP2.17. TRANSPORTATION SERVICES (B32.)

AP2.17.1. Student transportation costs, including daily commuting through military and/or contract transportation, and other transportation, as authorized by the DoDDS regional directors. Labor costs for DoD, U.S. or FN civilian bus drivers shall be based on the actual hours drivers are supporting school programs, plus 1 hour for cleaning the vehicle and performing driver's maintenance. To minimize costs, installation commanders shall use split-shift procedures and/or part-time personnel.

AP2.17.2. Rental and/or lease and operation of automotive vehicles in support of DoDDS activities.

AP2.17.3. Assignment of vehicles, materiels-handling equipment, and related equipment.

AP2.17.4. Transportation for dependents of military and civilian employees of the Department of Defense attending 5-day and 7-day dormitories, as authorized in Chapter 1., subsection C1.7.1.,above.

AP2.17.5. Civilian school bus monitors (when required by host-government statute), and school bus safety attendants (as authorized by the DoDDS).

AP2.18. UTILITIES (B.33.)

(Adjusted by the OUF.)

AP2.19. OTHER SUPPORT (B.35.)

AP2.19.1. Local drayage of household goods of DoDDS employees (not incident to permanent change of station) when directed by the U.S. Government (for example, when directed to move in, or out of, Government quarters).

AP2.19.2. Supplies and equipment obtained from the supporting installation supply accounts (except expendable medical supplies).

AP2.19.3. Packing and crating.

AP2.19.4. Rental of equipment required in support of authorized reimbursable services.

AP2.19.5. U.S. Government vehicle maintenance in support of DoDDS activities.

AP3. APPENDIX 3

NONREIMBURSABLE SUPPORT

The installation commander shall provide the following services, as available, to the DoDDS and DoDDS personnel on a nonreimbursable basis. DoDDS personnel shall be responsible for certain participation fees, registration fees, club dues, medical fees, and cost of purchases, on an individual basis.

AP3.1. CHAPEL AND CHAPLAIN SERVICES (A.1.) (EXCEPT CONTRACT CHAPLAIN/AND TEMPORARY DUTY COSTS)

AP3.2. COMMAND ELEMENT (A.2.)

AP3.2.1. Public information (the American Forces Radio and Television Service).

AP3.2.2. Public affairs.

AP3.2.3. Social actions (e.g., community services).

AP3.3. COMMON-USE FACILITY OPERATIONS, MAINTENANCE, REPAIR, AND CONSTRUCTION (A.3.)

AP3.4. DISASTER PREPAREDNESS (A.4.)

AP3.4.1. Noncombatant evacuation orders.

AP3.4.2. Explosive ordnance disposal.

AP3.5. ENVIRONMENTAL COMPLIANCE (A.5.)

Waste disposal, to include disposal of contaminated and hazardous materials, and other waste requiring special handling including any necessary receptacles.

AP3.6. FIRE PROTECTION (A.6.)

AP3.7. MORALE AND FITNESS SUPPORT (A.8.)

AP3.7.1. Recreation services (less payment of sports officials).

AP3.7.2. Common-use facilities such as base gymnasiums, recreational areas, and community support functions, such as bowling alleys, libraries, and recreation centers.

AP3.8. POLICE SERVICES (A.9.)

Law enforcement and/or police protection (unless DoDDS requirements are greater than the capability of the supporting Military Department installation to provide, such as when schools are physically located off-installation).

AP3.9. SAFETY (A.10.)

AP3.10. SHUTTLE SERVICES (A.11.)

Transportation by scheduled base and/or community shuttle bus.

AP3.11. ADMINISTRATIVE SERVICES (B.1.)

AP3.11.1. Mail pickup and delivery.

AP3.11.2. Processing of national Agency check (NAC) and investigations and personnel security clearances.

AP3.11.3. Administrative aspects of transportation, to include supervisors, dispatchers and other indirect cost personnel. That applies equally to supervision and administration of in-house operations or the monitoring and inspection of contractor and other third party operations.

AP3.11.4. Publications and forms supply, support, and services.

AP3.12. CLUBS (B.5.)

AP3.13. COMMUNICATIONS SERVICES (B.6.)

AP3.13.1. Military telecommunications (class A and/or C telephone, local and long-distance calls, and communication center).

AP3.13.2. Programmed lease and military long lines.

AP3.13.3. Leased long lines, if needed to provide class A service.

AP3.14. FOOD SERVICES (B.17)

Food service to include access to dining facilities to individual receiver personnel (individuals pay charges for items consumed) and school lunch program including cost of utilities, custodial services, and refuse collection.

AP3.15. HEALTH SERVICES (B.18.)

Outpatient medical services at the MTFs, if services were rendered under occupational health and safety programs or area-wide public health programs. The services include preappointment physical examinations and required immunizations. (Tuition-paying students are included.)

AP3.15.1. Enviromental Quality Control.

AP3.15.2. Occupational and Industrial Health Services.

AP3.15.3. Student-related medical services and expendable supplies provided to the dependents schools.

AP3.15.4. Veterinarian Service. DoDDS employees shall reimburse for individual veterinarian services.

AP3.16. HOUSING AND LODGING SERVICES (B.19.)

AP3.16.1. Family housing (DoD-controlled).

AP3.16.2. Housing referral service.

AP3.16.3. Bachelor Officers Quarters.

AP3.17. INSTALLATION RETAIL SUPPLY AND STORAGE OPERATIONS (B.21.)

AP3.18. LEGAL SERVICES (B.23.)

Legal services and/or claims and personal affairs.

AP3.19. MORTUARY SERVICES (B.26.)

Unless reimbursement is required and/or authorized in pertinent Military Service Departmental regulations.

AP3.20. TRANSPORTATION SERVICES (B.32.)

AP3.20.1. Transportation management and traffic management office services.

AP3.20.2. Terminal operations.

AP3.20.3. Transportation operator standby or dead time.

AP3.21. OTHER SUPPORT (B.35.)

AP3.21.1. Military labor.

AP3.21.2. Off-duty education services.

AP3.21.3. Search and rescue.

AP3.21.4. Aeromedical evacuation.

AP3.21.5. Open storage space, temporary storage, and real property.

AP3.21.6. Costs of schools officers and staff.

AP3.21.7. Drug abuse resistance education.

AP3.21.8. Any part of a foreign national's cost that is paid or reimbursed by the host nation.

AP3.22. <u>COMMISSARY SERVICES (C.1.)</u>

AP3.23. <u>EXCHANGE SERVICES (C.4.)</u>

    AP3.23.1. Exchange and motion picture services.

    AP3.23.2. Class VI stores.

    AP3.23.3. Officer and/or NCO club service.

    AP3.23.4. Aero and/or audio and/or photo clubs.

AP4. APPENDIX 4

COMPUTING LOGISTIC SUPPORT COSTS

AP4.1. GENERAL

This Appendix establishes procedures and provides operational guidelines for computing monthly costs of logistic and administrative support provided to the DoDDS. It also establishes standard reporting requirements for support category cost-formula computations to be provided with the monthly SF 1080 submission (or its Military Department equivalent) in those instances where unit and consumption factors can be quantified. That is similar to information that commercial activities in the United States (such as electrical companies) provide to their customers. Supporting documentation to validate DoDDS reimbursable costs shall include performance factors and the foreign currency rates used to convert local currency costs to dollars, when applicable. Explanations for adjustments to previously reported charges should also be provided. Both direct-cite and reimbursable costs shall be separately identified and included in those reporting requirements. All explanatory documentation in support of costs billed to the DoDDS may be subject to audit by DoDDS personnel.

AP4.2. ITEMS OF COST

Explanation for costing items of reimbursable support, keyed to specific categories, is provided in subsection AP4.2.1. through AP4.2.17., below:

AP4.2.1. Administrative Services (B.1.). That category includes administrative costs such as those incurred for briefings on installation policy, operation of supply and maintenance systems, personnel processing procedures, non-combatant evacuation orders, and alert plans; etc. While normally non-reimbursable, there may be exceptions to which both supplier and receiver have agreed. Identify cost and source.

AP4.2.2. ADP and/or Automation Services (B.3.). Reimbursable for direct costs for services provided to the DoDDS only.

AP4.2.3. Civilian Personnel Services (B.4.). Civilian personnel support charges shall be based on the net additional cost incurred (work-year equivalent effort required) by the supplier to provide the support. The total cost of civilian personnel support should be broken down by the number of DoDDS FN personnel supported and work hours devoted to that support. Costs of civilian personnel support shall be computed at a servicing ratio of 70:1 or a percentage factor based on actual numbers of DoDDS personnel supported derived from dividing the number of personnel supported by 70. In those cases where a different factor has been negotiated and documented in a MOU, the renegotiated factor shall be used.

AP4.2.4. Communications Services (B.6.). Charges to the DoDDS shall comprise the total costs of commercial telephone service and toll calls broken out by monthly service fees and individual toll calls. (Include number from which call was placed, if possible.)

AP4.2.5. Custodial Services (B.9.). The total reimbursable charges for custodial costs performed with in-house resources should be calculated for both the number of work hours and associated dollar costs of FN and U.S. civilian personnel. Reimbursable charges for the DoDDS shall be reduced by the applicable OUF. The number of hours worked each month times the average hourly pay rate for custodial personnel less any reduction for the OUF shall yield the DoDDS monthly cost. Costs for custodial services performed under installation or base-wide contract shall be based on square footage and associated labor for services devoted to the DoDDS. A breakdown of personnel costs by FN and U.S. civilian personnel is not required when custodial services are provided by contract performance. The DoDDS shall be charged for the cost of janitorial contracts that are solely for the benefit of the dependents schools, less any applicable reduction for the OUF. Excerpts from contract documents about DoDDS support and amendments, thereto, shall be provided to the school principal and to the regional office. Under either method of performance, the DoDDS shall be charged the cost of janitorial supplies, less any applicable reduction for the OUF. Charges for custodial services applicable to cafeteria support are the responsibility of the military installation and/or community. Those costs must be deducted from DoDDS custodial services costs besides deductions for the OUF.

AP4.2.6. Engineering Support (B.11.). That category of support shall be provided in accordance with the guidelines delineated in Chapter 5., above.

AP4.2.7. Equipment Operation, Maintenance and Repair (B.12.). That category includes the total amount of reimbursement requested for in-house support in supply, maintenance, and repair of Government-owned household appliances, furniture, furnishings, equipment, office-type furniture, and office equipment; such as calculators, reproduction equipment, typewriters, and specialty items for DoDDS schools program.

AP4.2.8. <u>Facilities and Real Property Support (B.14.)</u>. That category of support includes real property rentals. The DoDDS shall reimburse only those lease costs for permanent facilities and land, which are renewable annually and that are paid from O&M funds. Leases are subject to the OUF. A copy of the leases shall be provided to DoDDS personnel.

AP4.2.9. <u>Facility Maintenance and Repair (B.15.)</u>. That category includes the total cost, less application of the OUF, of real property maintenance, and repair for which reimbursement is being requested for school facilities. Maintenance personnel costs, maintenance supply costs, and costs of contract maintenance (or construction) shall be recorded on an actual basis. When repair and maintenance of school facilities is part of an installation-wide maintenance contract and actual cost data are not available, the DoDDS share of the total contract cost shall be based on proration of the square footage of the buildings maintained under the contract, less application of the OUF. THE DoDDS SHALL BE CHARGED FOR THE TOTAL COST OF GROUNDS MAINTENANCE. GROUNDS MAINTENANCE COSTS SHALL NOT BE PRORATED BY THE OUF.

AP4.2.10. <u>Finance and Accounting Services (B.16.)</u>. The charges for finance and accounting support shall be based on the net additional cost incurred by the supplier to provide the services. That cost should be broken down by the number of DoDDS civilian personnel supported and work hours devoted to that support. Accounting and finance activities, which support DoDDS regional office disbursements, should provide the total number of work hours expended processing DoDDS workload.

AP4.2.11. <u>Food Services (B.17.)</u>. Those charges shall include the number of meals served for dormitory students during the reporting period and the amount of reimbursement being requested for those meals.

AP4.2.12. <u>Laundry and Drycleaning (B.22.)</u>. That category should include actual costs of school and dormitory laundry and drycleaning to include draperies, sheets, and blankets. Personal laundry and drycleaning are not chargeable to the DoDDS.

AP4.2.13. <u>Printing and Reproduction (B.27.)</u>. The DoDDS shall reimburse for actual printing and reproduction costs incurred for the DoDDS. Cost of leased copiers shall not be included.

AP4.2.14. <u>Purchasing and Contracting (B.28.)</u>. That category includes the prorated salary of civilian personnel (over and above that required by the supporting activity) involved in purchasing and contracting for the DoDDS. An average contract cost of 3 percent for contract administration should also be included.

AP4.2.15. Refuse Collection and Disposal (B.29.). This category includes net additional identifiable costs for refuse collection and is subject to the OUF. Refuse collection and disposal for the school lunch program is not chargeable to the DoDDS.

AP4.2.16. Transportation (B.32.)

AP4.2.16.1. Daily Commuting. That category includes only the cost to transport students (including handicapped students) from their residence to school, for the start of normal school hours, and from school to their residence, immediately following the end of school hours. Students are authorized only one trip to and from school each day. Transportation for the noon meal, if provided, shall not be charged to DoDDS funds. The reporting requirements for that category of support include three distinct categories of cost; i.e., in-house operations, contract operations, and other transportation services. Other transportation services in support of various school activities including those outside normal school hours shall be reported under "Transportation Special Requirements (Curricular Activity Support)." Monthly billings to support transportation charges shall be computed in accordance with the following guidelines:

AP4.2.16.1.1. In-house Operation

AP4.2.16.1.1.1. Civilian Drivers. Charges for civilian drivers shall be computed in the following manner:

AP4.2.16.1.1.1.1. Determine the actual labor rate for the individual driver assigned, accelerated to cover the cost of the fringe benefits including leave. A command average or shop labor rate, similarly accelerated may be used instead of actual rates.

AP4.2.16.1.1.1.2. Determine the total work-hours to be charged by adding the actual hours that the driver(s) is engaged in school-bus daily commuting service (from time of dispatch until the time of return to the motor pool or assignment to another service other than daily commuting, whichever is first) plus up to 1 hour each day for operator maintenance and cleaning of the vehicle.

AP4.2.16.1.1.1.3. Determine the actual cost to be charged by multiplying the total hours by the labor rate.

AP4.2.16.1.1.2. Supervisors, dispatchers, and other indirect-cost personnel constitute administrative aspects of transportation services and, as such, are nonreimbursable. That applies equally to supervision and administration of in-house operations, as to the monitoring and inspection of contractor or other third party operations.

AP4.2.16.1.1.3. Charges for safety attendants assigned to special education daily commuting services shall be computed, as follows:

AP4.2.16.1.1.3.1. Determine the actual hourly rate for each employee or the average hourly labor rate for safety attendants employed. The basic salary rate shall be accelerated to cover all applicable fringe benefits.

AP4.2.16.1.1.3.2. Determine the work hours to be charged. While the basic rule would parallel that for driver time, from departure from motor pool until return to the motor pool, it may be necessary for other circumstances to allow additional items; e.g., 2 hours in the morning and 2 hours in the afternoon as minimum employment periods.

AP4.2.16.1.1.3.3. Multiply the work hours by the applicable accelerated labor rate(s).

AP4.2.16.1.1.4. Charges for automotive equipment utilized in student transportation services shall be based on:

AP4.2.16.1.1.4.1. A per-mile rate by type of vehicle developed in accordance with regulations of the Military Department. The rate shall compensate the supplier for equipment maintenance and operation (including fuel), other than operation labor. The cost of equipment (variously termed "investment," "depreciation," or "replacement") shall not be included in the per-mile rate. The rate may be developed either for the individual military community or for all communities under a military subordinate command.

AP4.2.16.1.1.4.2. The actual miles equipment is operated on daily commuting services may be determined from the odometer readings logged by the operator at the beginning and end of each service. For scheduled services, mileage may also be calculated by multiplying the measured route distance, including deadhead travel to the first and from the last service point each day, by the number of days on which service was required during the charging period.

AP4.2.16.1.1.4.3. The cost to be charged for equipment shall be determined by multiplying the total actual miles by the per-mile rate.

AP4.2.16.1.1.5. Operational Data

AP4.2.16.1.1.5.1. Number of Buses. The monthly documentation should include a breakout to show the minimum number of Government-operated vehicles (buses, sedans, and/or carryalls) required to provide the scheduled daily commuting services. Do not include vehicles held in reserve or used to replace vehicles temporarily out of service.

AP4.2.16.1.1.5.2. Number of Bus Runs. The total number of daily trips to and/or from school should be reported. For example, transporting a busload of kindergarten students to school in the morning and from school at midday would be two trips even though just one vehicle was utilized.

AP4.2.16.1.1.5.3. Number of Students Transported. Supporting documentation should show the number of students who are authorized use of Government-operated commuting services. Each student shall be counted no more than one time. The total number of students reported plus the number of students residing in the designated walking area, should not exceed the actual enrollment of the school(s) covered.

AP4.2.16.1.1.5.4. U.S. Civilian Drivers. Show the average number of U.S. civilian drivers employed on schoolbus commuting services each day by the supporting organization. Also include the total number of work hours, which U.S. civilian drivers worked on daily schoolbus commuting services during the period covered.

AP4.2.16.1.1.5.5. FN Drivers. Show the average number of non-U.S. drivers employed each day by the supporting organization and the total number of work hours that non-U.S. drivers worked on daily commuting services during the period.

AP4.2.16.1.1.6. Contract Operations

AP4.2.16.1.1.6.1. DoDDS funds shall be cited on the contract. The actual costs shall be based on the contracted service rate multiplied by the number of times and/or units the service is required, less any reductions made for unsatisfactory performance or failure to perform. Costs of scheduled services shall be segregated as to daily commuting, curricular, and co-curricular, based on the purpose and designation of the specific service. Costs for safety attendants for authorized special education services shall be separately identified and reported.

AP4.2.16.1.1.6.2. If the bus service contract incorporates services other than DoDDS commuting routes, contract costs shall be prorated based on miles operated, or equipment hours, in service.

AP4.2.16.1.1.6.3. The costs of transportation management, contract inspection, quality control, and administration aspects are not authorized charges to DoDDS funds.

AP4.2.16.1.1.6.4. Operational Data

AP4.2.16.1.1.6.4.1. Number of Buses. Show the minimum number of contractor vehicles (buses, sedans, and carryalls, etc.) required to provide the daily commuting services contracted. Do not count reserve or standby vehicles.

AP4.2.16.1.1.6.4.2. Number of Bus Runs. Show the number of daily commuting trips operated by the contractor-operated daily commuting services.

AP4.2.16.1.1.6.4.3. Number of Students Transported. Show the number of students who are authorized to use contractor-operated daily commuting services.

AP4.2.16.1.1.7. Other Transportation Services. The actual costs of other transportation services shall be charged to DoDDS funds.

AP4.2.16.1.1.7.1. Public Transportation. (Rail, intercity bus services, and municipal mass transport services.) Those services may be procured in advance by the supporting organization or procured by the student and/or sponsor subject to reimbursement by the Government. Care must be exercised to procure that transportation at the most economical cost feasible; e.g., monthly student pass, commercial, or reduced-rate bulk issue tickets, etc.

AP4.2.16.1.1.7.2. <u>POVS</u>. In certain situations, it may be cost advantageous to the U.S. Government to authorize transportation of students(s) by a POV to the school or a central pickup point, subject to reimbursement of the student and/or sponsor at the standard authorized rate as established in the JFTR, volume 1 and the JTR, volume 2 (references (r) and (s)).

AP4.2.16.1.1.7.3. <u>Taxi</u>. In some limited circumstances, and for limited periods of time, parents, guardians, or sponsors may arrange for transportation of their dependent children by taxi, subject to reimbursement of expenses. In each of the situations in subparagraph AP4.2.16.1.1.7., above, care must be taken to obtain specific approval before the service is utilized.

AP4.2.16.2. <u>Special Requirements - Curricular and Co-Curricular Activity Support</u>. That category includes the costs of all student transportation in support of school activities including those held outside normal school hours. It also includes the cost of bus monitors, where required by host-nation statute, and cost of administrative transportation required for support of the school program and/or staff. That support may be provided by in-house operations, contract performance, or, in limited circumstances, privately procured services subject to reimbursement. The method of support shall normally be the same as that provided by daily commuting. DoDDS policy limits special transportation to major population centers and/or central transportation points such as bus and rail stations. Those trips shall normally be limited to one trip each day and shall include stops only when a minimum of four, or more, students are being discharged.

AP4.2.16.2.1. <u>Curricular Transportation</u>. Curricular transportation consists of student transportation services in direct support of school curricular and school events during the normal school day. Participation in curricular activities is mandatory rather than voluntary and is normally scheduled for an entire class. Included in that category are the following:

AP4.2.16.2.1.1. Study Trips.

AP4.2.16.2.1.2. Services in support of cooperative work experience assignments.

AP4.2.16.2.1.3. Shuttle or other services between a school and a remote annex, or to facilities such as a gymnasium, swimming pool; etc., not located near the school.

AP4.2.16.2.1.4. Services for one-time requirements such as high school orientation visits, graduation practice, and school participation in a local community event; etc.

AP4.2.16.2.2. Co-Curricular Transportation. The following services are authorized in support of DoDDS with co-curricular activity programs:

AP4.2.16.2.2.1. Transportation between school and activity and/or event location.

AP4.2.16.2.2.2. Transportation to and/or from athletic, or other, facilities not available at school.

AP4.2.16.2.2.3. Transportation leaving school in the late afternoon, at the end of the activity period, to central drop-off points; or transportation to school, before regular daily commuting services, to use practice facilities not otherwise available. The cost of providing curricular and co-curricular transportation shall be computed, as described in subsection AP4.2.16., above, for daily commuting services.

AP4.2.16.2.2.4. Bus Monitors and Safety Attendants

AP4.2.16.2.2.4.1. School Bus Monitors

AP4.2.16.2.2.4.1.1. In-House. Report the number of civilian monitors and associated salaries when those are authorized charges to the DoDDS funds.

AP4.2.16.2.2.4.1.2. Contract. Report the number of bus monitors authorized and provided under contracts and the actual cost of those services.

AP4.2.16.2.2.4.2. Safety Attendants

AP4.2.16.2.2.4.2.1. In-house. Report the number of safety attendants authorize by the DoDDS and associated salaries.

AP4.2.16.2.2.4.2.2. Contract. Report the number of safety attendants authorized and provided under contracts and the actual cost of those services.

AP4.2.16.2.2.5. Dormitory Student Transportation

AP4.2.16.2.2.5.1. Report number of 5-day dormitory students and their transportation costs by all transportation modes between dormitory school and primary residence.

AP4.2.16.2.2.5.2. Report the number of 7-day dormitory student dependents of DoD military and civilian employees, and their transportation costs, by all modes between dormitory school and primary residence.

AP4.2.16.2.2.5.3. Dormitory Activity Travel. Report the number of students and costs for authorized transportation (other than that reported under subparagraphs AP4.2.16.2.2.5.1. and AP4.2.16.2.2.5.2., above, in support of dormitory students.

AP4.2.16.2.2.6. Administrative Vehicles

AP4.2.16.2.2.6.1. Administrative Transportation. Report cost to the DoDDS of Government-owned or -leased administrative vehicles. If a vehicle is on long-term loan from the motor pool, indicate the DoDDS prorata share of maintenance and/or operation costs. If a vehicle is leased for the DoDDS, report the monthly lease cost, if known, or one-twelfth of annual lease cost. If vehicle is assigned to the DoDDS from a motor pool for a one-time service, report the cost charged to the DoDDS computed, in accordance with subparagraph AP4.2.16.1.1.4. above.

AP4.2.16.2.2.6.2. Taxi and Shuttle Service. For official business use only. Specify basis on which charges are assessed and total charges.

AP4.2.17. Utilities (B.33.). When separate meters or separate heating plants for the school facility exist, the actual cost of utility service shall be used. All metered utility costs shall be reduced by the applicable OUF. When utility services at the school facility, or facilities, are prorated among all users, the reimbursable cost shall be computed for each category, as follows. Utility costs factored with the formulas in paragraphs AP4.2.17.1. through AP4.2.17.5. , below, reflect DoDDS costs for use of the utilities during the school day. When using the formulas in paragraphs AP4.2.17.1. through AP4.2.17.5., below, the OUF shall not be applied.

AP4.2.17.1. Water (Unmetered). The following water consumption factors shall be used:

Water Unmetered

Type of Facility	Consumption
School	15 gal each person each school day
Dorm (only residents)	55 gal each person each dorm day

The school population figure shall include students, teachers, instructional aides, and full-time administrative personnel. The principal shall supply that information on request.

EXAMPLE

This example assumes a population of 189 students and 11 teachers and administrators, or 200 total, and a unit price of water at $0.11 per 1,000 gallons. Total consumption and cost computation are, as follows:

Example

Average Population		Consumption Factor		Actual School Days This Reporting Period		Reporting Period Consumption
-------------	X	----------------------	X	------------------------	=	----------------------
200		15		51		153,000 gal

Periods						
Consumption	/	1000	X	Unit Price		Cost Each Period
153,000	/	1000	X	$0.11	=	$16.83

(1,000 U.S. gallons = 3.7854 cubic meters. There are up to 183 instructional days each SY, but actual school days in the period covered by the report are to be used.)

AP4.2.17.2. <u>Sewage</u>. A factor of 70 percent of the total gallons of water consumed by the school for the period shall be used for the amount of sewage disposed. In isolated instances, local governments may bill the supporting Military Service more than 70 percent. When the actual usage varies from the standard 70 percent rate, the percentage used to determine sewage disposal cost may be changed after the supporting installation has shown supporting documentation. Those instances shall be approved by the DoDDS regional director. The percentage rate times the unit price for sewage disposed shall give the school sewage charge.

AP4.2.17.3. <u>Electricity</u>. An illumination factor of 3 watts each square foot each hour shall be used to determine the use for school purposes. A 7-hour day shall be used for that computation when elementary and/or intermediate and/or middle schools are involved, and an 8-hour day shall be used when either junior or senior high schools are involved. Those computations shall include air conditioning, unless the installation has a separate air-conditioning plant. If that is the case, compute DoDDS costs based either on the metered amount or the prorated charge. This example assumes the total area of the elementary school facility is 20,000 square feet and the electricity unit price is 0.25 dollars each kilowatt hour (KWH).

Electricity

Square Feet		Illumination Factor		Actual School Days This Period		Hours Used Each Day		Reporting Usage
---------	X	---------------	X	---------------------	X		=	
20,000		.003		51		7		21,420 KWH

Period Usage	X	KWH Unit Price	=	Cost Each Period
21,420	X	0.025	=	$535.50

AP4.2.17.4. <u>Heating Fuels (Gas, Fuel Oil, and Solid Fuels)</u>. When the school has its own heating facility, the cost of fuel shall be reimbursed. When the school is heated from a central plant, reimbursement shall be based on the proportion of school space heated to the total amount of building space heated by the central plant. Engineers and/or public works officials shall reduce the amount of fuel and labor costs chargeable to school operations by the OUF to compensate for use of the school by other users.

AP4.2.17.5. <u>Miscellaneous Utilities Costs</u>. Those costs include reimbursable labor involved in firing school boilers or for visits of roving operators, if the plant is oil-fired. Labor costs chargeable to the school, whether the school has its own heating facility or is heated from a central plant, shall be reduced by the OUF to compensate for use of the school facility by other users.

AP4.2.18. <u>Other Support (B.35.)</u>

AP4.2.18.1. <u>Subsistence</u>. Reimbursement for subsistence shall be in accordance with the procedures negotiated between the school and the commissary officer.

AP4.2.18.2. <u>Expendable and General Supplies</u>. That category includes costs incurred for expendable, nontechnical commodity materials provided in support of the DoDDS, wherein the ISA is the authorizing document.

AP4.2.19. <u>Fire Protection (A.6.) and Police Services (A.9.)</u>. Fire protection and police services are routinely provided on a nonreimbursable basis. Under certain circumstances, installation commanders may incur net additional identifiable police service costs in support of the DoDDS. In those instances, and with prior approval of the regional director, the DoDDS may be charged for police support above and beyond that which would be provided by the installation for other tenants. Only those costs are reimbursable and included under that category of support.

AP4.2.20. <u>Other Costs</u>. Identify other costs and include the applicable two-position category of support codes used on the ISAs.

AP4.2.21. <u>Total Logistic Support Charges</u>. The grand total should represent all costs associated with the support of DoDDS activities, including those funded through direct citation of DoDDS funds.

(<u>REMARKS</u>. Provide the names and mailing addresses of supporting activities) and the school(s) supported, and the FY and month in which the support was provided. Also, provide the name, rank and/or grade, phone number, and organization of the individual who prepared the report. Reference the applicable ISA number and associated MIPR number(s). The information should be documented on plain white paper and be attached to the monthly billing.)

(<u>NB</u>: Monthly costs less than 500 dollars may be accumulated and billed quarterly or annually, in accordance with DoD 7220.9-M (reference (t)).)

AP5. APPENDIX 5

U.S. NAVY SUPPLY SUPPORT OF DEPARTMENT OF DEFENSE OVERSEAS DEPENDENTS SCHOOLS

AP5.1. PURPOSE

This Appendix prescribes policy relative to supply support of the DoDDS.

AP5.2. SCOPE

The policies and procedures prescribed in sections AP5.3., AP5.4., AP5.5., and AP5.6., below, apply to all U.S. Navy installations designated as the support activity for the DoDDS. Those schools may be located on, or near, the Navy support activity installation.

AP5.3. REFERENCES

AP5.3.1. DoD Instruction 4000.19 (reference (c)).

AP5.3.2. NAVSUP PUB 437 (reference (u)).

AP5.3.3. NAVSUP Manual, Volume II (reference (v)).

AP5.3.4. MOU (reference (w)).

AP5.3.5. NAVCOMPT Manual, Volume III (reference (x)).

AP5.4. RESPONSIBILITIES

The policy guidance and procedures promulgated in DoD Directive 1342.6 (reference (a)), references (c) and (u) through (x) shall be used when the designated Navy installation provides support to the DoDDS. The installation commander, through subordinates, and with school officials, is responsible for the following:

AP5.4.1. Appointing an installation dependents school's officer in accordance with this Manual to act as the liaison between administrators and installation Agencies in discharging school support responsibilities for those categories of support covered by the ISA, generally covering administrative, logistic, supply, and maintenance support.

AP5.4.2. Processing all National Stock Numbered (NSN) and/or non-NSN material requests, in accordance with the NAVSUP Pub 437 and the NAVSUP Manual, Volume II, references (u) and (v), called for by the terms of the MOU, reference (w) and this Manual. The installation commander shall provide technical assistance and advice to the school administrators on all supply matters about dependents schools.

AP5.4.3. Ensuring that the budgetary augmentation to support nonreimbursable school requirements for the support of the school program are included in installation funding and/or budget documents and are submitted through normal budgetary channels for inclusion in local O&M budget estimates and financial planning. Refer to this Manual for logistic support reimbursable budgeting information.

AP5.5. SUPPLY AND ACCOUNTING PROCEDURES

AP5.5.1. The NSN material shall be requisitioned and turned in through the supply department, in accordance with standard Navy procedures, using the DD Form 1348-1, "DoD Single Line Item Release/Receipt Document," format. Material requirements shall be filled from supply department stocks when available. When retail stocks of requested items are not available at the field level, the supply department shall pass the requisitions on to the Navy supply support activity or integrated materiel manager, in accordance with standard procedures. Dependents school requisitions qualify for the same force activity designator as the installation supporting activity.

AP5.5.2. Non-NSN materiel (school-unique) shall be requisitioned by schools, in accordance with Chapter 4., above.

AP5.5.2.1. Normal distribution shall be made for bulk quantities of textbooks and supplies by utilization of surface transportation through the military ports. Where items in limitedquantity are procured, transportation, i.e., air or surface, shall be utilized based on the most economical method commensurate with the issue priority designator established by the supporting activity.

AP5.5.2.2. Shipments of annual requirements shall be made to ensure arrival at the supporting activity or school before August 1.

AP5.5.2.3. Local arrangements shall be made between the supporting activity and the school official for physical delivery of school supplies and equipment to the dependents school, if required.

AP5.5.3. Appropriation and cost accounting shall be in accordance with NAVCOMPT Manual, Volume III (reference (x)). Installed equipment in the DoDDS shall be accounted for, in accordance with reference (x).

AP5.6. ISAs

AP5.6.1. The ISA between the supporting activity and the school shall be prepared, in accordance with DoD Instruction 4000.19 (reference (c)) and this Manual.

AP5.6.2. Besides the categories prescribed by (reference (c)), the ISA shall include specific provisions for the storage of school material and equipment and turn-in of excess materials (NSN and non-NSN).